TH_ STORY OF WRITING

ABCDEFGHI
JKLMNOPQR
STUVWXYZ
a b c d e f g h i j
k l m n o p q r s

by Gail K. Gordon
illustrated by Cynthia Watts Clark

PEARSON

Scott
Foresman

Editorial Offices: Glenview, Illinois • Parsippany, New Jersey • New York, New York
Sales Offices: Needham, Massachusetts • Duluth, Georgia • Glenview, Illinois
Coppell, Texas • Ontario, California • Mesa, Arizona

CONTENTS

Chapter 1
What Is Writing?

Your cat stares at the refrigerator and meows. Her meows are not words as you know them, but you recognize their tone. It's the "feed me now" tone. Is she speaking "cat," a language you understand but cannot speak?

Cats and other animals can communicate with each other—and sometimes with us—but they are not using a language when they do. At least, they do not have a "language" in the way that human linguists define language.

To rise to the level of language, communication must have rules. These rules are part of a system called grammar. While we may understand the cat's message, it is not possible for cats to combine sounds in new ways that express new thoughts. A cat cannot write. Language and its visual representation—writing—belong only to human beings.

We know that cats can communicate with us, but not in words.

No one knows how old language is or exactly how it developed in human communities. Evidence suggests that the earliest writing system may have developed about 6,000 years ago. Even though we might not know how it first developed, we can guess that as human society became more complicated, our ancestors must have wanted to communicate more complicated ideas. Simple grunts and cries would not have been clear or specific enough. As language developed, social interactions and communication could become more complex. Likewise, as society continued to develop, so did language. Even today, as our society changes, our language changes with it to meet new needs.

In the chapters that follow, we will see how different systems of writing developed and technological developments had an impact on writing. The history of writing is not a simple story to tell, but like most stories about human society, it is an interesting one.

Chapter 2
The Earliest Writing: Cuneiform

Cuneiform, what we call the earliest form of writing, was developed more than 5,000 years ago. Archaeologists have found thousands of clay tablets with cuneiform in the remains of Sumerian settlements.

The Sumerians lived a settled life, not a nomadic one. They were farmers and shepherds with cattle and sheep, and were the first people to build cities. They needed a way to keep records of trading and laws. Since the Sumerians lived in one place, there was time for a writing system to develop.

Cuneiform means "wedge-shaped." This writing looks like lines and wedges in different combinations.

Archaeologists believe that the Sumerians' first writings were trading records. In the earliest stage of the development of cuneiform, simple pictures were used to represent things that people saw every day. A picture of a goat meant one goat.

As the writing system developed, the pictures became even simpler, so that the scribe, or writer, could draw the symbol in fewer strokes. These simple drawings are called pictograms.

The pictograms were drawn on soft clay tablets with a sharpened reed. The tablets were then baked in ovens or dried in the sun until they hardened.

At first, the pictograms were drawn in vertical columns. Later, they were drawn in horizontal rows. This made the writing of the characters easier, as did a new writing stylus. With the new stylus, the wedge-shaped characters could be created more easily and quickly.

Eventually, it was not enough to simply use a pictogram to refer to an object. People wanted a way to express less concrete thoughts; they began to produce what we call ideograms. As their name suggests, these symbols could refer to abstract ideas, such as happiness, as well as concrete objects. This was a great leap forward, but there was another leap yet to come.

Early cuneiform pictograms went through stages of development. They became simpler and sometimes changed direction.

Cuneiform pictograms and ideograms were reasonably easy to produce and to read, but there were more than 2,000 symbols! That meant that few people could become true masters of the skill of writing. This limitation led the Sumerians to develop phonograms.

Phonograms are linked to the sound of the spoken language. In the modern English language, *ock*, as in *clock*, and *oke*, as in *joke*, are phonograms. Combined phonograms called "rebus devices" were used to represent the sound of a word.

Scholars believe that this change from one system to another happened gradually over time. The signs became more simplified. The scribes still needed to learn about 600 phonograms, but that was fewer than before.

Chapter 3
Writing in Ancient Egypt: Hieroglyphics

At the same time the region of Mesopotamia was writing with cuneiform, Egypt was using a writing system called hieroglyphics.

Scholars think the development of hieroglyphics may have been influenced by cuneiform. It is believed that traders and other travelers may have carried cuneiform clay tablets with them from one place to another in their **caravans.**

The earliest hieroglyphic inscriptions are from the same period as cuneiform writing—about 5,000 years ago. However, some scholars think that hieroglyphs may have begun even earlier because the system was so well developed. Egyptian scribes recorded stories as well as ideas about law, medicine, and agriculture in hieroglyphics.

The word *hieroglyphic* comes from the Greek language. It means "holy carving."

Egyptians used papyrus sheets that served them as paper serves us. Papyrus is a reed that grows along the Nile. It was also used to make ropes, mats, and even sandals. The Egyptians cut the stems of the plant into thin strips and placed them on top of one another at an angle to produce a strong surface. Scribes used a reed to write on the papyrus with black ink made from soot and water and red ink made of cinnabar, a reddish mineral, and lead oxide, a reddish compound of lead and oxygen.

Drawing hieroglyphs on paper took too much time and skill to be used every day. The scribes working with ink on papyrus developed a cursive script that allowed them to work more quickly. They called it hieratic.

Eventually a third script came into use called demotic script—"writing of the people." Demotic could be written even more quickly.

Texts in hieroglyphics do not easily give up their secrets. Usually, a text reads from right to left, but there are exceptions. For example, the text might change its direction, running right to left in one line and left to right in the next or even top to bottom in one column and bottom to top in the next.

Visitors to exhibits of ancient Egyptian artifacts can admire the beauty of hieroglyphic inscriptions and learn what the texts say by reading scholars' translations. Scholars have made much use of the Rosetta Stone. Discovered by French soldiers in 1799 in the Egyptian village of Rashid, the Rosetta Stone is written in hieroglyphics, demotic, and Greek. In 1822, a linguist used it to discover the grammar of hieroglyphics. This allowed him and all the scholars who followed to uncover the meaning of the writings on the stone.

The Rosetta Stone is in the collection of the British Museum. It was the key for scholars to the secret of reading hieroglyphics.

Chapter 4
In China: Ancient Characters

In China, a writing system developed approximately 1,000 years after the writing systems of Mesopotamia and Egypt. Remarkably, that same system—with only minor changes in some characters—is still used in China today. Only the technology of writing has changed.

In spoken Chinese, many single syllables sound the same and carry more than one meaning. Listeners use both tone and context to understand the meaning of words. The Chinese never developed a purely phonetic, or sound-based, system of writing. Like other writing systems, Chinese writing began as pictograms and ideograms that were simplified over time.

Most modern characters are also made up of a root that suggests the meaning and another sign that suggests the sound. Chinese characters appear in columns or rows. In order to read a Chinese newspaper, a reader would need to know several thousand characters.

The Chinese writing system serves many versions of the language. Chinese speakers who do not understand one another can read the same texts. This ability to share writing has helped to unify Chinese culture.

When the computer revolution began, writers of Chinese faced a challenge. An alphabet system requires only one byte of computer memory, but a Chinese character takes two. This problem was solved, and today Chinese writing can be rendered electronically.

Like hieroglyphics, Chinese characters are appreciated for the beauty of their form. They are often an important element in Chinese art.

Chapter 5
Our Alphabet: Those Familiar ABCs

Most experts agree that the alphabet we are familiar with began about 3,000 years ago with the Canaanites—also called the Phoenicians—who lived along the Mediterranean Sea. The Phoenician alphabet was a phonetic system, but it contained only consonants. Around the same time, Aramaic developed, as well as Arabic and Hebrew writing, which are phonetic systems that probably have their roots in the Phoenician alphabet.

The Greeks used the Phoenician-based consonant signs and borrowed consonant signs from Arabic to represent vowel sounds. After about 2,500 years, the Greeks had an alphabet of 24 letters, many of which we would recognize today.

The Greek alphabet seems to have been the source of the Latin alphabet, our own "ABCs." Like the Phoenicians, the Greeks were sailors and probably spread the use of their alphabet through trade.

The writing system used in this book came to us from the Romans, who wrote in Latin. Although other European languages were spoken, all official documents were written in Latin. It was not until the year A.D. 842 that an official document was written in the language of the people. It was a treaty written in Old German and in Old French.

During **medieval** times, monks wrote in Latin, the language of the church. They produced beautiful, hand-written **manuscripts** with illuminated letters and illustrations.

By the time of the Renaissance, more people outside of monasteries were learning to write. A scribe might be paid by a wealthy **patron** to produce documents. A historian might record the **legacy** of a king. An astronomer could record the stars seen from his **observatory.** Books about many subjects began to appear, but they could not yet be mass produced. They were written one at a time and only the very wealthy could afford to own them.

Chapter 6
The Printed Word

When books were first introduced, printers tried to imitate the hand-lettered pages produced by scribes. These books were large and expensive both to make and purchase.

In the fifteenth century, Johann Gutenberg invented the first mechanized printing press. By the end of the sixteenth century, books were being printed in spoken languages, not just in Latin. Printed letters replaced hand-drawn letters, and some printers began to produce smaller books. These smaller books were more affordable and easier to carry.

Johann Gutenberg changed the way books were produced when he invented the printing press.

As printing technology for books advanced, people wondered if handwriting would eventually disappear. It did not. At an early age, even children of today study the art of penmanship.

In the nineteenth century, inventors experimented with pen design and formulas for ink. In 1945, the ball-point pen was produced in great numbers. Today the ballpoint is still used, but now we also have soft-tipped pens and inks of many colors.

In advancing from the pen to the typewriter, people wondered again if handwriting would disappear. Today we use computers, and some people wonder if one day we might do all of our reading from computer screens.

Handwriting is unlikely to disappear. People seem to feel comfortable using writing tools, and new hand-held electronic devices allow us to write on a screen as if we were writing on paper.

From clay tablet, to papyrus sheet, to modern paper, to the computer screen, the written word has appeared on many surfaces. It has served as a **beacon** shining both into our past and our future—revealing history and allowing us to explore our hopes and dreams.

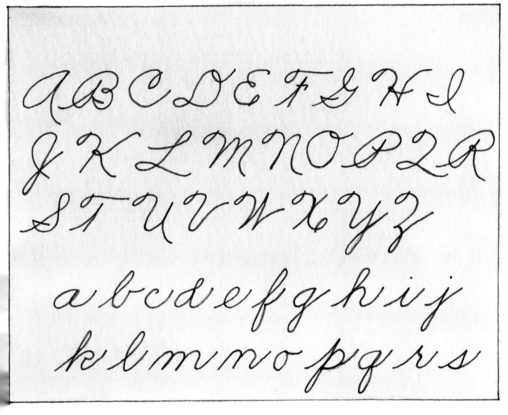

The Palmer method became a popular method of handwriting instruction in the late nineteenth century. It was common in classroom instruction well into the twentieth century.

Glossary

beacon *n.* a source of light or inspiration.

caravans *n.* groups of travelers on a journey often with animals; trading expeditions.

legacy *n.* something inherited or received from an ancestor or a time in the past.

manuscripts *n.* documents written by hand.

medieval *adj.* related to the Middle Ages in Europe, from the fifth to the middle of the fifteenth century.

observatory *n.* a building that provides a good view of the sky.

patron *n.* someone who gives money or other support, usually to an artist.